WHERE WAR LIVES

A Photographic Journal of Vietnam

DICK DURRANCE

WHERE WAR LIVES

A Photographic Journal of Vietnam

DICK DURRANCE

Introduction by Ron Kovic

THE NOONDAY PRESS · NEW YORK
A division of Farrar, Straus and Giroux

Library of Congress Catalog Card Number: 88-7226
Published simultaneously in Canada by Collins Publishers, Toronto
Typeset in the United States
Printed and bound by Dai Nippon in Japan
Designed by G.M. deLesseps
First edition, 1988

Although a helicopter crash recently took Bill Weems from us, I still feel his hand on my back, urging me to reach for those pictures imagined but not yet captured. For his unfailing encouragement I dedicate this book to him, a beloved and missed friend

ACKNOWLEDGMENTS

THERE ARE A NUMBER of individuals I wish to thank for their special contributions to this book: Craig Stevens for giving generously of his vast technical knowledge when I ran into difficulties printing the negatives; Mike deLesseps, for believing in the photographs from the earliest prints and for creating a design that allows the pictures fully to reveal themselves; Tennyson Shad, for conveying to Roger Straus III his enthusiastic response to the pictures; Roger Straus III, managing director of Farrar, Straus and Giroux, for so quickly embracing the idea of publishing the images as a book; Steve Wasserman, editor and publisher of Hill and Wang and Noonday Press, for his clear judgment and seamless editing in guiding the book to its full potential; Laurel Frye, for seeing to it that the project moved forward even when commercial assignments took me to far crannies of the world; and Bonnie Durrance, my wife, for her support and her astute editorial reviews, which contributed vitally to the shape of the book. In addition, I want to express my appreciation to Jobo Fototechnic Inc., whose processing equipment helped maintain a consistent quality among the prints and to The Maine Photographic Workshops for support throughout the project.

UNITED STATES OF AMERICA

CONTENTS

We used to wonder where war lived,
What it was that made it so vile.
And now we realize that we know where it lives,
that it is inside ourselves.

ALBERT CAMUS

WHERE WAR LIVES

FOREWORD

In 1966 I went to the army as a young man hoping to serve his country and as an aspiring photographer hoping to capture on film insights into the nature of war. At induction I convinced the drill instructors to let me take pictures as they stripped us of our hair and clothes and issued us dog tags and fatigues. I photographed as we reached across vast cultural differences to make friends in never-ending lines of strangers, and I carried my camera as drill instructors force-marched our bodies into shape and unleashed instincts for violence we did not know we possessed.

As a photographer in the Department of Army's Special Photographic Office (DASPO), I flew all over Vietnam, from the DMZ to the Mekong Delta, photographing operations with units as diverse as the helicopter-borne 1st Air Cavalry Division and the floating Mobile Riverine Force. My personal Nikon F, swathed in tape to protect it from dust, went everywhere with me. The pictures I shot with it were like notes for a journal, so the photographs were not colored by an editor's needs or a project's point of view. They were simply an instinctive response to the heart-stopping terror of patrolling a jungle trail in the Que Son Valley or to the grisly horror of fighting our way through tiny villages like Tan Toi Nhut.

Much of combat is beyond the power of images or language to convey. No words exist to describe the eerie quiet in Da Nang the first morning of the Tet Offensive. Walking back through the outskirts of the city after taking leave of the forces chasing NVA invaders, my buddy and I realized that the neighborhood was apparently deserted. The only visible occupants were two women, evidently killed on their way to market, lying dead in the street. Perhaps the invaders we had been chasing were not out in the rice paddies, where the rest of the troops were still searching, but in tunnels right under us. Never have I felt so vulnerable. The few pictures I took that morning convey an ironically peaceful mood. What I remember feeling is a stark terror.

Prior to the Tet Offensive, I often wandered through the Vietnamese communities adjacent to our bases. While I seldom felt confident that I was among friends, I rarely sensed immediate danger. Rather, I felt a wary ambiguity in their response. Dressed in my jungle fatigues, I probably appeared to them both as an opportunity for a quick piaster and as an oppressor, the soldier of yet another foreign army come to fight in their country.

When I was released from the army, I printed a sampling of the images. They won several trophies from the National Press Photographers Association, and two prints were selected for the *Popular Photography Annual.* But I was anxious to put Vietnam behind me and to get on with my budding career as a photographer for the *National Geographic.* So I put the pictures away, hoping the memories of combat would fade. For twenty years I ignored the pictures and the experiences they depicted.

Then I, like so many others, saw Oliver Stone's movie *Platoon.* I went home and pulled from the attic a dusty box of photographs. The negatives were stained and scratched, the victims of careless storage and terrible processing conditions in Vietnam. The story they tell is the universal tale brought back from all wars. One senses that the feelings expressed by the men I photographed, in spite of their modern weapons, like helicopters and M-16s, were not much different from those known to warriors fighting in the Peloponnesian War two thousand four hundred years ago.

Dick Durrance

Introduction

There is nothing in the lives of human beings more brutal and terrifying than war and nothing more important than for those who have experienced it to share with us its awful truth. Within this simple yet eloquent collection of photographs by Dick Durrance you will find the story of a generation of Americans who went to war and what they witnessed there. One of the first photographs in this book reminds me of my own induction into the United States Marine Corps at Whitehall Street in New York City in September of 1964. I was eighteen years old and I remember leaving my house in Massapequa, Long Island, saying goodbye to my mother and father, telling them how proud I was to be serving my country. I had never forgotten that beautiful winter's day in 1961 when President Kennedy had told us that the torch had been passed to a new generation of Americans and that we would have to be willing to bear any burden, suffer any hardship for the cause of freedom. I still remember raising my hand at the induction center that day, with all the other innocent boys, proudly repeating the oath of enlistment, thinking of President Kennedy, and my mother and father, and all the people who would be proud of me someday, and all the things I would do for my country. Like myself, the kids in that photograph grew up with John Wayne and the Hula Hoop, Sputnik and Eisenhower, Kennedy and the New Frontier. Like myself, they played stickball in the streets in front of their houses, read *Boys' Life*, and climbed trees and wrestled with their brothers and got yelled at by their mothers, and prayed and played hooky and lied and cheated and stole and loved and dreamed a million different dreams. Look closely at their faces; they had their first job last summer and they kissed a girl for the first time last week. We're all there together in that photograph—black and white and Puerto Rican, farm kids, city kids, and boys from the suburbs, all having grown up in America and having played Cowboys and Indians and eaten Wheaties in that fall of 1964, that last moment of innocence when everything would change forever. Only a short time later, some of us would be dead and others would come home wounded like myself in a wheelchair for life.

I was wounded in Vietnam on January 20, 1968, while leading my squad across an open area. I was shot through the right foot, the bullet passing through the front of my foot and blowing out the back of my heel. I could not walk anymore and fell to my knees, where I continued firing my rifle and crawling forward in the sand under heavy fire. Just as I started to get up, I took a bullet through my right shoulder. I heard the crack next to my right ear, and it sounded like a firecracker. Suddenly I felt nothing from the mid-chest down. My body seemed to have been blown in two. I reached back with my hand and felt to see if I was still intact. My body seemed to have gone up in the air and had disappeared or was suspended in back of me, above my head. A man came running up to get me and I screamed for him to stop. But he kept coming, and there was a loud crack, and I heard him scream and moan, and then die right behind me, shot through the heart. I remember the intensive-care ward, drifting in and out of the morphine, and people dying all around me. And I returned home, where I have lived with that war every day for the last twenty years in my wheelchair and where I will live for the rest of my life.

In the many months I spent in the hospital after being wounded, I had time to think about all the things that had happened, and I began to question why I and the others had gone to the war in the first place. We were warriors long before we went to boot camp, long before we flew in an old DC-3 to Raleigh, South Carolina, and from there boarded a bus to Parris Island. In our back yards, we fought against our friends, imagining them to be Japs and Germans. We played war, making the sounds of explosions and rifle fire with our mouths, imitating the war we saw on television and read in the Sergeant Rock comics and watched in the movies every Saturday afternoon. We had marched and shot and killed, bayoneted and strangled and murdered countless men, and it had all been make-believe. Now we were being given a chance to do it for real. This was our opportunity to put all our play into practice.

Boot camp was a turning point, the place where boys were made mean. Even today, I remember the sound of men running on the parade deck, the thumping of their boots, and I hear them shout in cadence: "Kill Vietcong! Kill Vietcong!" "If I die in a combat zone, box me up and ship me home—one, two, three, four; one, two, three, four!" I see the drill instructors, the DIs, in their perfectly starched utilities, their spit-shined boots and utility caps, their thin waists and brightly sparkling buckles. They run alongside the formation past the barracks now, sergeants and staff sergeants arrogantly and proudly undefeated and so sure, strutting. We are in charge. We are the DIs. Your new fathers and mothers. Listen up, scumbags! We will do your thinking for you now. We are your conscience now! We will be miserable and mean to you here only because we want you to be your best in combat. We want you to kill and be a fighting machine. We want you to murder your enemy, to get his blood on your hands, to feel it wet and cold, to smell its sweet aroma, to stick a knife deeply into his back, twisting it upward into his frightened heart, as you kill him silently, without a scream. We are in hell, and we are breathing. We're getting you ready for war, boys, for the killing and the dying, for the fighting and the fucking, and you'd better listen up or you're gonna be dead.

I remember the DI drove one kid crazy and he committed suicide, jumping out of the second-story barracks window after they had tormented him for weeks, calling him a "Jewboy," and opening his letters from his mother and his girl back home, reading them aloud to all the men in the squad bay. There were others, too, who drowned trying to escape the madness through the swamp, and still others who somehow miraculously got away. I thought of running away and dreamed of what it might be like, but never took the chance, too afraid of what might happen to me. I was frightened most of the time, too scared to admit to anyone, even the priest, what I was feeling.

The weeks and months passed, and I graduated and finally left the island. I remember the graduation ceremony and how we marched together that day with our drill instructors, all in perfect step. I can still hear their voices, calling cadence on that morning so many years ago. I remember there was a formation and a speech by a lieutenant colonel which I have long since forgotten, and how proud I felt that day as I stood on the parade deck. That afternoon we left on a bus and were sent to Camp Lejeune, North Carolina, where we were taught advanced combat infantry training. We learned to throw the hand grenade and fire the bazooka, all the weapons of war.

I returned home, on leave, on December 24, 1964, and I remember my sister and I went shopping that night, Christmas Eve. I lied to my parents, telling them boot camp had been a great experience, and I acted as if I had really grown up. I tried to stand taller when I walked around the house and speak in a deeper voice as if I was a man. I played the good Marine for them and all the neighbors. I went down to the high school and showed off my new uniform and spit-shined shoes. I walked proudly around the halls, hoping the girls would notice me. Later I walked all the way back to my house from the high school so the whole town could see me. Deep down inside, I knew I had made a mistake, but what could I do? I had already signed the papers. I was in for the next four years, and I decided to make the best of it, to be the finest Marine I could be. The following Christmas I would be in Vietnam, thirteen thousand miles from my home.

There is a photograph that is classic and timeless, of boys on the beach with their fresh, clean uniforms on and their seabags by their side. They have arrived at their destination. They are a generation about to go to war, kids from Des Moines and Biloxi, St. Paul and Mobile, New York and Los Angeles, the sons of truck drivers and farmers and factory workers. They are the young men of the working class, and some will never be the same again. It is an important day in their lives—the day of their arrival in the war. They seem so sure and confident and proud. And why not? America was the most powerful nation in the world. We had never been defeated. But on that beach in that photograph, all of that is about to change.

I remember the day I arrived in Vietnam, grabbing my seabag and walking off the plane into the tremendous heat that hit me like a wall. In the distance, a few ARVN soldiers, their caps tipped back on their heads, M-1 carbines in their hands, were on the runway, seemingly taking a lazy stroll. As I marched toward the hangars in my shiny boots and new uniform, my clean rifle in my hand, I saw others with gaunt, hollow stares, torn fatigues, mud-caked boots, rumpled clothing. They were going home. They had done their time. They looked old and tired, beaten by something we had not yet experienced. We were their replacements —"the new guys." We did not realize what it meant to be in this place. This is Vietnam, I remember thinking. I was excited. I had made it to my first war. It was December 1965, and I was surprised that no one shot at us when we landed. I wondered where the war was that I wanted so badly to find. I wanted desperately to prove that I was a good Marine.

It is difficult for me to look at these photographs, to relive what I and millions like me went through. Many of them seem to sum up everything that is true and terrible about war. Look, for example, at the photo of boots sitting atop sandbags. They are the boots of war, the boots we wore and walked through the rice paddies with. These "jungle boots," cracked and unpolished, with their green-canvas porous sides, are probably drying in the sun, a soldier asleep in his bunker, exhausted from some patrol the night before. I wore boots like these on both my tours of duty in Vietnam, when I was in Recon and would have my trousers tightly tucked into my boots to keep the leeches out, and when I was stationed on the mouth of the Cua Viet River and it rained all the time and my feet were always wet, and when I was shot just before the Tet Offensive. They were comfortable boots, lightweight, not like the heavy leather boots we wore in boot camp. They still look familiar to me, and I guess they always will. Not long after I was released from the hospital, I went into a sporting-goods store in my hometown and I remember seeing the boots in the photograph for sale. They were clean and brand-new, neatly polished. I was angry. How could anyone now buy the boots we had worn in the war, the boots that Sergeant Botiger had worn the day he was blown apart by an artillery shell, the boots I wore the day I was paralyzed from the midchest down? I thought of buying a pair that day, and even asked one of the clerks if he would take them down from the shelf so that I could look at them. And I held them in my hands, thinking thoughts and feeling things I knew no one in the store could ever understand.

Look carefully at the photographs of men in combat, especially the one of a tank or an APC moving through the shattered remnants of what was once a village. The trees seem to be screaming as if trapped in some nightmare from which they cannot awaken. The sky looks evil, and you can almost hear the terrible sound of engines screeching and groaning above the roar of gunfire. There is a photograph of a boy with a hard look on his face. Behind him, a human skull rests atop the barrel of an M-16. He has killed now and entered a world different from our own, and he reminds me of the time when the men came back from patrol, displaying in a glass jar the fingers they had cut off the Vietcong they had killed. I remember feeling sick inside, and outraged. Another photograph shows a soldier sitting on a sandbag and others in a truck. They look tired. They have brought in two bodies, perhaps VC killed along a riverbank after having been flushed out of caves in which they were hiding. Now they are being brought into the command post for the captain to look at. I remember seeing bodies like these. They resembled frozen statues of death, their eyes staring out of their heads in great fright. I remember that the jaw of one man drooped and his head and neck were twisted backward. There were two small bullet holes in the chest and his whole back had been blown out in a shred of blood and guts. Our bullets had turned the Vietnamese boy inside out. I forced myself not to be concerned. I'm in a war and he's the enemy, I told myself. The body didn't look human anymore, and I never once thought that that body covered with mud could be me someday. I was a Marine. I was tough. I could take it. It was my job. I couldn't wait to get more Vietcong; this was only the beginning.

I thought and daydreamed that afternoon about what it would be like to kill a man, how it would feel to pull the trigger to take a life out of the world, to blow away another human being, to blow away a gook. I'll do it, I thought; if I have to, I'll do it. I remember the time the captain set fire to the woman's hooch with his Zippo lighter; she was screaming and crying, and had her baby in her arms. I remember how bad I felt. This isn't right, I thought. We were sent over here to help these people. But I watched in silence, trying to be a good Marine, as the woman's home burned to the ground, together with everything she owned, because the captain thought she was sympathizing with the enemy. The men from my platoon kicked in large clay pots of rice, scattering the foodstuffs of the village all over the ground. Then they urinated on them. Many hooches were burned that day. The whole village was set ablaze. We were angry. A number of our people had hit booby traps. The day before, a lieutenant had gotten his foot blown off, and so we gathered up VC suspects, young children and old women, even a blind man.

What we saw on patrol and what we had been taught war would be like seemed to be two different things. I'd fantasize I was John Wayne in *The Sands of Iwo Jima*. Maybe that black soldier in the photograph with the machine gun over his shoulder thinks he's Audie Murphy in *To Hell and Back*. Or the gunny sergeant with the serious look on his face taking a drag from his cigarette as he readies himself to go out on patrol. Maybe he's humming "The Star-Spangled Banner" to the loud roar of the chopper blades, the way I did when we would lift off from the LZ and head out on patrol. I'd hum all the way to the drop zone where, all painted with camouflage, we'd jump from about ten feet into the elephant grass, diving out of the open doors of the helicopters with our 75-pound rucksacks on our backs and rifles in our hands, five M-26 hand grenades taped to our cartridge belts. We'd take a deep breath. We're going in, yeah, just doing our job, just keeping busy for a couple of days out here in North Vietnamese territory. Got our maps and binoculars, got our claymores and compasses, got our pop flares and air support. Just out here to do a little snooping and pooping to see what old Charlie's up to, Victor Charles, that is, we respect him, you know. We're Recon, the best, we can take the heat and the mosquitoes, and the leeches that drop from trees like raindrops thudding into the leaves. I remember waking up one morning with one attached to my testicle, and I had to pull it off, and how bloated it had become sucking the blood from me all night long.

Sometimes it was so hot and the pack and radio I carried on my back were so heavy I thought I wouldn't be able to make it, but you kept walking, past the Vietnamese working in the rice paddies. You looked at them with suspicion. You tried to remember you were in a war. You saw the water buffalo, and the bomb craters from the B-52s which made you feel as if you were on the moon. I remember a pig that had been killed by shrapnel from one of the bombs, and how the lieutenant laughed, and as the men walked past the pagoda, they kicked the pig again and again, and the smell of incense was in the air. There was a funeral procession, and a statue of Buddha was broken in two. Someone had smashed it with his rifle butt, just to let them know the Americans had arrived. There was crying from babies, and barking from dogs, the smell of shit and strange food cooking, and always the feeling you were in a place very far from home, walking in someone's back yard, pissing and shitting on their front lawn. They'll understand, and if they don't, it doesn't matter: they're only gooks. Nobody thinks about Kennedy anymore. They just count their days.

Another day and maybe I will come home alive. A letter from home: Dear Son. The world, back where it's real and green, where I can breathe again, where my family is, where my town and everything precious to me is. Why am I so far away? What is this place? What are we doing here?

Among the most disturbing photographs are those of prisoners being interrogated. In one photograph there appears to be an American, perhaps an intelligence officer, with a .45 pistol clutched in his right hand, a camera slung around his neck. A cigarette is stuck in his mouth, and he looks as if he would shoot the prisoner without hesitation if he thought he could get away with it. The prisoner, a young Vietnamese, seems to be pleading for his life. Another American soldier, perhaps a sergeant, has his hand on the prisoner's neck, gripping it tightly. Another Vietnamese, the interpreter, holds two rifles and listens to the prisoner's pleas. There is a look on his face, nearly a scowl, of indignation. He is almost laughing. He wants to make the Americans proud of him. He is calm, murderously calm, while the officer with the .45 is very angry. Perhaps he lost a man the other day to a booby trap, or to a sniper, or perhaps he has been patrolling for days and his men are just sick and tired of being harassed by an enemy no one can seem to find. Now this man is the scapegoat. What is taking place is, in a sense, a court proceeding; more precisely, an inquisition. The prisoner is guilty until he proves he is innocent. That is the way it is in war: the gun against the head, the prisoner talking excitedly, trying to save himself from certain death. How many times has this happened in other wars, in other places, with other men?

There is a photo that bothered me very much. I had a nightmare after looking at it for the first time. It is the tent of the dead. There are body bags and stretchers on the outside of this makeshift mortuary. There is a sign that says "Keep Out." Dead American boys are inside. If you look at no other photograph in this book, I want you to look at this one, because this is where war lives. It lives in that tent, and it is grotesque. And it is silent. And it stinks from decay. Inside are the bodies of the boys who stood on the beach only a few months before. Go back and look at that photo of the men on the beach. They are the ones who are now in the tent, they are dead, and soon they will be prepared as the dead are for their return home. Do not go into that tent, because you will see war in there. You will see something horrible and dishonorable. You will see war in its most awful consequence. You will see the warriors, but you will not like them. For once you see them in that tent before they have been readied to look good and smell clean again, before their holes are patched up and their bloody garments replaced, before their angry stares have been removed, their eyelids pressed down to hide their last scream for life, to cover up their rage at having to leave this world so soon—you will know where war lives. This is the tent of the dead, where the blood is mopped off and the intestines are put back into place for the long journey home. This is where the man I killed was sent, where his body was fixed up and prepared to be sent home, the man that I killed in that instant of indecision, in that moment of panic and doubt. I pulled the trigger and took a life from this world, so sure he was the enemy. How wrong I was that night. I killed my own man by accident. Now he lies in that tent. To kill another human being is to kill a part of yourself. The bullet has pierced my throat also, and I am bleeding. I am in the tent, too. In that tent lies a human being I hardly knew, a man from Georgia under my command. I was the squad leader. His life was in my hands, the hands that held the gun, the finger that pulled the trigger. I killed an American by mistake. I thought he was the Vietcong. I didn't kill the enemy I was taught to kill. If I had killed a Vietnamese, would it have made any difference? I was taught to kill. I shot; he fell. Now he lies in the tent. In a mirror I now see his face in my reflection. I know now where war lives. It is cold and I am shivering and I dream of redemption, of forgiveness, of healing and love. I know I must keep on living. I know I must try. I try to believe again, even in the darkness of this angry room.

The photographs don't end here. There are soldiers writing letters home; men absurdly playing baseball in the middle of the war; men in the whorehouse catching clap; men on R&R, drunk and arrogantly walking the street of another country they know nothing about, past people they do not even see as people. We did not know that those we had been sent to protect and save would be the ones we would kill and maim. I met a young Vietnamese boy on my first tour. His name was America. He must be in his thirties now, if he's not dead. I wonder what became of him. I wanted to help him. I told him we came to save his country from communism. I spent the whole day with him. He really liked me. I wonder if he ever thinks of me. And the boy whose foot we shot off by mistake? I wonder where he is tonight. I wonder who his mother is, and if she would like to talk to me. They hated us that night for murdering their fathers and sons. When, the following morning, the lieutenant told me that the people we had killed and wounded were VC, I did not believe him. They were civilians, I told him—innocent people we thought were the enemy. I told him I was sick of going out on patrol, that it was hard to tell who the enemy was anymore. Body count was all that mattered.

There is one photograph that almost defies description. It is so horrifying I want you to look at it, to study it carefully, especially you politicians and patriots of all countries that send men to war. Stick your nose down into this photograph and inhale the remains of this once-human being, his decapitated body scattered on the ground, an arm here, a leg there, a torso. Look at it carefully, please, you who say wars must be fought, and men must die, you who play the marching tunes and give the speeches, you who build the monuments and write the glorious history of men in battle. Look at this unknown representation of humanity with the rope around his wrist, his bloodied arm, his torn chest. Look into his eyes staring up in fright, his mouth screaming, even in death. This is the face of war. This is what is hidden in that tent. This is the son you bore, the child you held in your arms and promised always to love and cherish. Look at this photo carefully. Someone killed that man, and someone killed him in a terrible way. He is crying in that photograph, even in death he is crying and pleading, telling us where war lives. His is the silent scream of the dead.

Those of us lucky enough to have survived the homecoming after the trauma of our injuries yearn for life now, for beauty, and all that is decent and good, for in war we saw the worst in the human being. We saw poverty and death, killing and savagery, the darkest sides of the human soul, the most hated parts of our humanity. We who have taken our wounds and our sorrows and chosen to make them stand for something better have an obligation to rise above our pain and anguish, to turn the tragedy of our generation into a triumph and learn from the errors of our fathers and ourselves. No one knows peace or the preciousness of life better than the soldiers who fought in war, or those who have been affected by it directly: the mother of a son who has died, a wife who will never see her husband again, a child who will never have a father, a father who will never see his son again. For it is we who have lived with the physical and emotional scars of war, we who have lived with these wounds every day and felt, every morning, their weight and pain. It is we who have walked and wheeled through the streets of our country and watched children stare at us and wonder why. And it is we who cry out now for the future, for a world without war. We are the reminders of what war can do, of how it can wound and hurt, and diminish all that is good and human. We struggle every day to believe in a life that was almost taken away from us. We know that even though we have lost, though parts of our bodies may be missing, though we may not be able to see or feel, we are important men and women with important lessons to teach, with important things to share.

I know war very well. I know it in the night when I am sleeping and nightmares still come. Or in the morning when I wake up and get into my wheelchair to start my day. I am very happy to be alive, and recently I bought a piano and hope to learn to play it someday. I love to play the high notes; they are gentle and soothing to me, almost like the sound of raindrops on my window when I was a boy. Just to touch the keys from time to time helps me to forget the war. The music of the piano fills the air with healing. The past recedes. And sometimes even the nightmares disappear for a while. The sound of a single note gives hope. Somehow we must begin to find the courage to create a better world, even if it is with one note or one step.

RON KOVIC

I Transformation

ONE

Induction

WELCOME
TO THE
UNITED STATES
ARMY

19

TWO

Basics

A

DUYGO
U.S. ARM

U.S. ARMY

McCREADY

THREE
Skills

2

WEBB
U.S. ARMY

Biscayne

II War Zone

FOUR
Combat

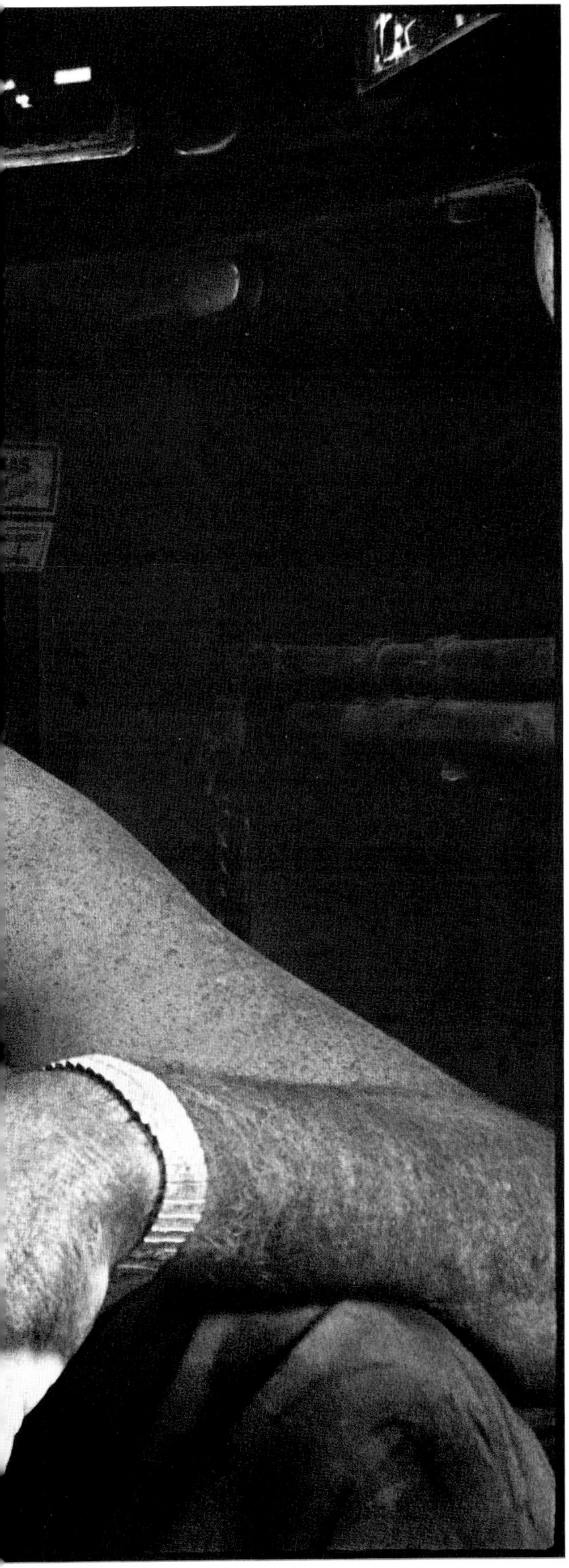

FIVE
Warriors

200 CARTRIDGES
7.62MM NATO M13
CARTONS
1 M62-4 M80
FUNC LOT LCL. 104668
(A131)

U S ARMY
4L 8925
C
09

SIX
Patrol

SEVEN
The Rear

REGISTRATION
UNAUTHO
PERSONNEL
KEEP OUT

HỚT TÓC
LÊ HỮU
TÂN MỸ TRANG
NAM NGUYÊN

Honda 50

III Victims

EIGHT
Civilians

HEM 6
HEM 6
TAXI
TAXI
NAD 968
NBI 798

VIỆT-NAM NGÂN
THE SAIGON POST
L.B.J. Westy Discuss Troop Need
Daily News
L.B.J. faces open revolt in Congress
MELIA

XE ĐẠP XE GẮN MÁY
KHÔNG ĐƯỢC VÀO ĐÂY

NINE
Children

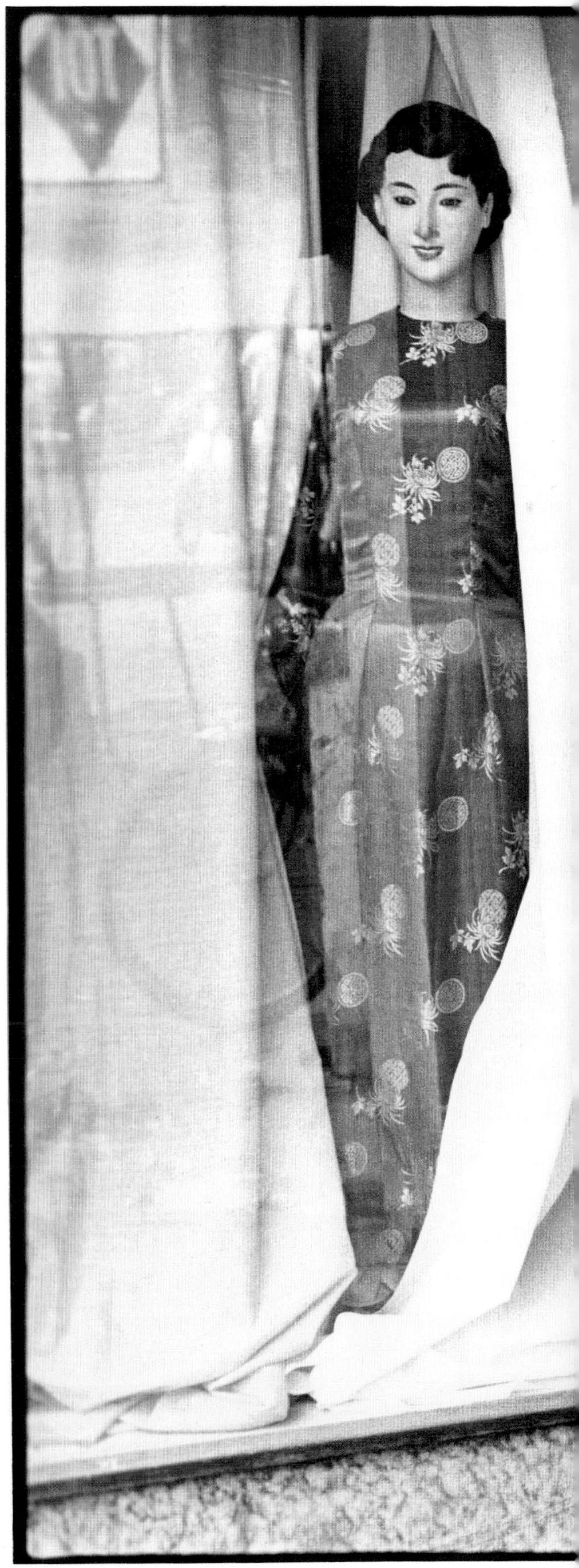

Coca-Cola
Coca-Cola

KIỂU HỢP THỜI

THỤY
HÂN

IMPORTED
Keiller
ORANGE DROPS
PRODUCT OF GREAT BRITAIN
3 x 10 LB. BAGS
Coca-Cola
Coca-Cola

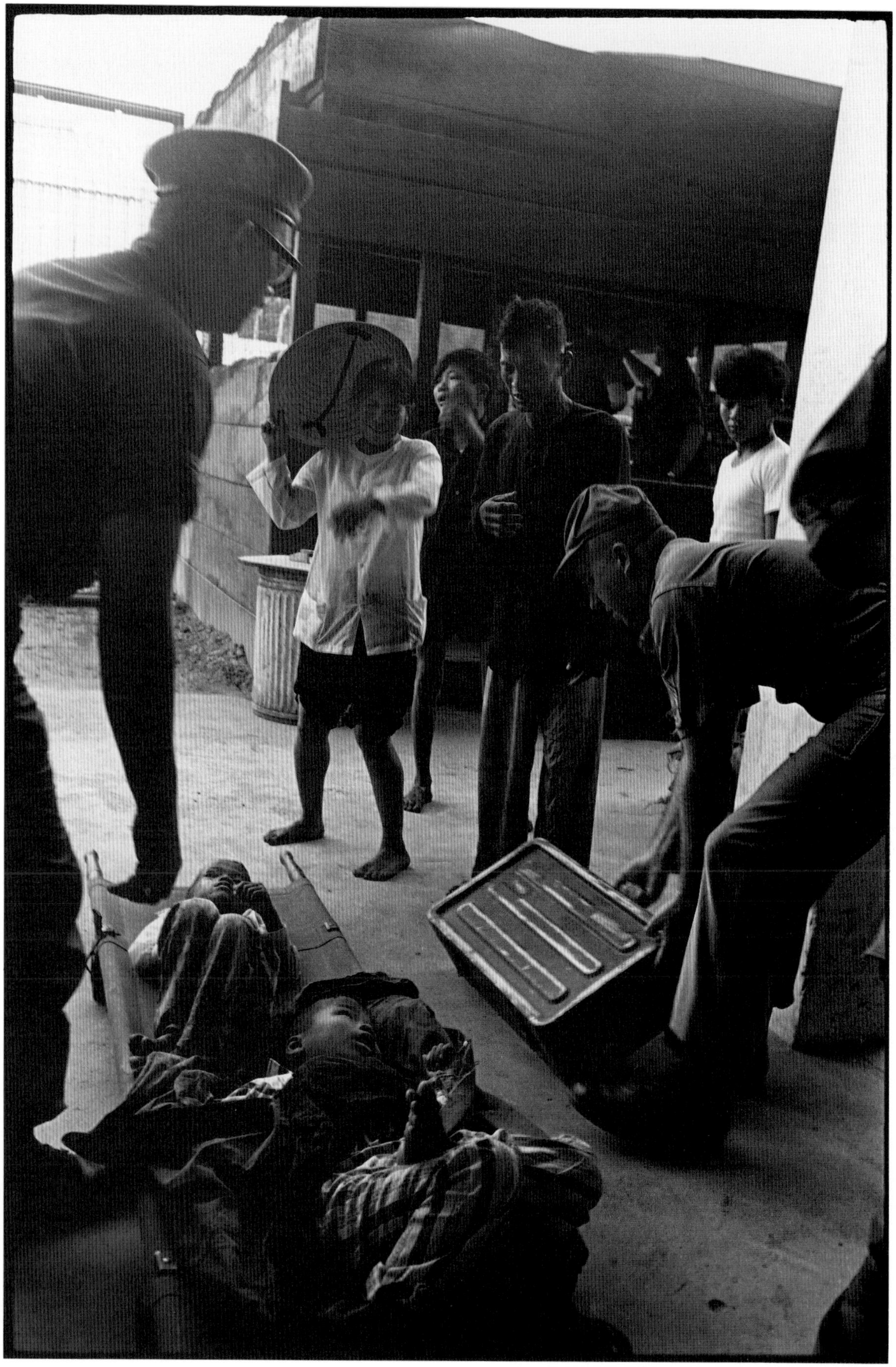

TEN
Casualties

AFTERWORD

I HAD BEEN LIVING with these pictures for three months, studying and printing them, when the tears came. I think it was the eyes staring from those young, rapidly aging faces that broke my numbness. Their expressions seemed to reflect emotions and questions I had avoided for years. The tears that came were quiet and few, but they rose from a source deep in my memory. It was not so much for myself that I cried, but for all of us who went to Vietnam.

I wondered what became of the men I photographed. Did they survive? Intact? Or did some of them, like Ron Kovic, suffer physical wounds that will never heal? How many are still trying to recover from the psychic horror of fighting an enemy they rarely saw or discovering that the shadow they felled was a child? For some, I am sure the memories have proven a more tenacious enemy than the North Vietnamese.

Their expressions seem to reflect a shock such as I felt on my first encounter with body bags. Nothing in our upbringing prepared us for the horror of zipped-up remains —dead dreams wrapped in olive-drab, rubberized silence.

Nor did our training tell us how to regain control over the instinct for killing unleashed in basic training. What were we supposed to do with those skills when we returned to the world? How were we to deal with the discovery that the impulse was ingrained in our natures, not imposed by the drill instructors?

Most of us, I think, ran from that impulse. I flew off to a photographic assignment in Rumania within two weeks of being discharged, and have been circling the globe as a photographer since. Running toward my next assignment, I never confronted these unanswered questions.

In the course of printing these pictures, I finally opened myself to the deeply buried grief for friends lost in Vietnam and I allowed myself to acknowledge the violence now lying dormant but not extinct within me.

Nothing can repair the damage caused by war, but returning to the memories and pictures has connected me to those experiences, which, in spite of my efforts to ignore them, have done so much to shape the rest of my life.

List of Photographs

40–1 Firing range, Ft. McClellan, Ala., September 1966.

42 Live-fire course, Ft. McClellan, Ala., September 1966.

43 Firing range for .50 machine guns, Ft. McClellan, Ala., October 1966.

44 Truck ride, Ft. McClellan, Ala., October 1966.

45 Jumping from truck at rifle range, Ft. Jackson, S.C., August 1966.

46 Award ceremony, Ft. Jackson, S.C., August 1966.

47 Weekend visitors, Ft. McClellan, Ala., October 1966.

48–9 Graduation parade, Ft. McClellan, Ala., November 1966.

52–3 Troops stepping ashore at Vung Tau, August 1967.

54–5 M-60 tank and M-113 armored personnel carriers (APCs) of B Troop, 3/4 Cavalry, 25th Infantry Division, in firefight at Tan Thoi Nhut, a village 5 k. NW of Tan Son Nhut air base, Saigon, March 1968.

56 Elements of D Company, 1st Battalion, 27th Infantry, 25th Infantry Division, helping soldier wounded in firefight at Tan Thoi Nhut, a village 5 k. NW of Tan Son Nhut air base, Saigon, March 1968.

57 Squad leader, D Company, 1st Battalion, 27th Infantry, 25th Infantry Division, reassembling his troops after firefight in which the squad suffered one man killed and three men wounded at Tan Thoi Nhut, a village 5 k. NW of Tan Son Nhut air base, Saigon, March 1968.

58 Elements of D Company, 1st Battalion, 27th Infantry, 25th Infantry Division, taking shelter in trench after firefight at Tan Thoi Nhut, a village 5 k. NW of Tan Son Nhut air base, Saigon, March 1968.

59 Medics treating member of D Company, 1st Battalion, 27th Infantry, 25th Infantry Division, wounded in firefight at Tan Thoi Nhut, a village 5 k. NW of Tan Son Nhut air base, Saigon, March 1968.

60-1 Elements of D Company, 1st Battalion, 27th Infantry, 25th Infantry Division, moving past house destroyed in firefight at Tan Thoi Nhut, a village 5 k. NW of Tan Son Nhut air base, Saigon, March 1968.

62–3 Crewman, M-113 armored personnel carrier (APC), B Troop, 3/4 Cavalry, 25th Infantry Division, Tan Thoi Nhut, March 1968.

64 Gunner and assistant gunner, M-113 armored personnel carrier (APC), 2nd Brigade, 25th Infantry Division, Cu Chi, March 1968.

65 Infantryman, 1st Battalion, 12th Infantry, 2nd Brigade, 4th Infantry Division, Camp Warrior, Pleiku Province, July 1967, at his tent with skull he found on a patrol.

66 Infantryman, 1st Air Cavalry Division, carrying M-60 machine gun on road approaching LZ Stud, Quang Tri Province, March 1968.

67 Montagnards serving in the Army of the Republic of Vietnam (ARVN) aboard a CH-47A (Chinook) helicopter near Pleiku, August 1967.

68 Perimeter guard, 1st Air Cavalry Division, Camp Evans, March 1968.

69 Squad of perimeter guards, 1st Air Cavalry Division, driving to their duty stations, Camp Evans, March 1968.

70–1 Artillerymen, A Battery, 6th Battalion, 33rd Artillery, 1st Air Cavalry, LZ Stud, March 1968.

72 Door gunner, UH-1B helicopter, 1st Air Cavalry Division, carrying his M-60 machine gun after mission, Camp Evans, January 1968.

73 Door gunner, UH-1B helicopter, 1st Air Cavalry Division, firing M-60 machine gun on mission near Camp Evans, January 1968.

74–5 Crewman, CH-47A (Chinook) helicopter on mission over Mekong Delta, August 1967.

76–87 Elements of A Company, 5th Battalion, 7th Cavalry, 1st Air Cavalry Division, on a patrol in the Que Son Valley, Quang Nam Province, Operation Wheeler–Wallowa, January 1968.

88–9 Jazz group, Camp Evans, January 1968.

90 Body bags outside graves registration tent, Camp Evans, January 1968.

91 Award ceremony, location unknown.

92 Baseball game, Camp Evans, January 1968.

93 Pet monkey, Camp Evans, January 1968.

94–5 Artilleryman, A Battery, 6th Battalion, 33rd Artillery, 1st Air Cavalry Division, LZ Stud, Operation Pegasus, March 1968.

96 House of prostitution, location unknown.

97 Location unknown, possibly Pleiku.

98–9 Altercation, Saigon, August 1967.

102–3 Location unknown, possibly near An Khe.

104 Women digging irrigation ditch with piece of discarded military equipment, Binh Dinh Province, July 1967.

105 Military and civilian traffic, Saigon, August 1967.

106–7 Pimp and prostitute, Vung Tau, August 1967.

108 Saigon street scene, August 1967.

109 Cyclo driver, Saigon, August 1967.

110 Shopkeeper, Saigon, July 1967.

111 Shopkeeper, Saigon, July 1967.

112 Location unknown.

113 Farmers planting rice, Mekong Delta, August 1967.

114–15 Location unknown.

116–17 Girl in dress shop, Saigon, August 1967.

118 Girls and mother outside beauty parlor, Saigon, July 1967.

119 Refugees at temporary shelter, Saigon, February 1968.

120 Boy scavenging, Cholon district of Saigon after Tet Offensive, February 1968.

121 Girl playing beside barricade, Saigon, July 1967.

122 Boys wounded in Tet Offensive arriving at hospital, Saigon, February 1968.

123 Member of A Company, 5th Battalion, 7th Cavalry, 1st Air Cavalry Division, playfully marking forehead of Vietnamese boy with unit's designation.

124 Boy who had lost both legs, at rehabilitation center, Saigon, February 1968.

125 Boys playing cards, casket shop, Saigon, August 1968.

126–7 Resident, Cholon district of Saigon, after Tet Offensive, February 1968.

128 Women washing clothes, Cholon district of Saigon, after Tet Offensive, February 1968.

129 Cholon district of Saigon after Tet Offensive, February 1968.

130 Woman examining contents of trunk after fire destroyed her home, Saigon, February 1968.

131 Firemen fighting fire in home, Saigon, February 1968.

132–3 Home destroyed in firefight, Tan Thoi Nhut, a village 5 k. NW of Tan Son Nhut air base, Saigon, March 1968.

134 Woman killed on the first morning of the Tet Offensive, Da Nang, January 30, 1968.

135 Women wounded on the first morning of the Tet Offensive, Da Nang, January 30, 1968.

136 Girl killed on the first morning of the Tet Offensive, Da Nang, January 30, 1968.

137 Women in temporary shelter, refugee camp, Saigon, February 1968.

138–9 Charred remains, first morning of the Tet Offensive, Da Nang, January 30, 1968.

141 Nun, orphanage, Cu Chi, March 1968.

142 Specialist 4th class Dick Durrance II, Department of Army Special Photographic Office (DASPO), in bunker at Camp Evans, March 1968. Photographer unknown.

A Note about Dick Durrance

Dick Durrance was born in Seattle in 1942, and educated at Phillips Academy, Andover, and Dartmouth College. He served in the U.S. Department of Army Special Photographic Office in 1967 and 1968, documenting military activities in Vietnam, Thailand, and South Korea. In 1969, Durrance joined the photographic staff of the *National Geographic*. Seven years later, he left the magazine for a career in corporate and advertising photography. His work has won many awards, including the Advertising Photographer of the Year (1987) award, given annually by the American Society of Magazine Photographers. He lives in Rockport, Maine.

A Note about Ron Kovic

Ron Kovic, a former U.S. Marine who served two tours of duty in Vietnam, is the author of several books, including *Born on the Fourth of July*.